Ros Stephen

Violin Junior

A Creative Violin Method
for Children

Concert Book 2

ED 23122
Online Material available

Illustrations by Ulrike Müller

www.schott-music.com

Mainz · London · Madrid · Paris · New York · Tokyo · Beijing

SCHOTT

About this Book

- This collection of pieces complements Violin Junior Lesson Book 2.

- The pieces cover a wide range of styles from classical to folk and world music and are ideal for concert performances or additional repertoire.

- Piano accompaniments, with chord symbols for guitar or accordion, are included for all pieces in an extra part.

- Violin accompaniments are included in the book as alternatives to the piano accompaniments.

- Several canons and duets are included to encourage ensemble playing.

- Audio recordings of every piece (performance and play-along tracks) are available to download from www.schott-music.com/online-material (see below).

- Audio files are also available on streaming services.

Have fun!

Ros Stephen

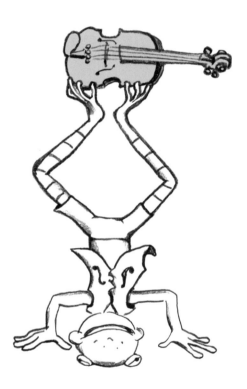

  Please visit **www.schott-music.com/online-material**
to download all audio files for free using the following voucher code: **fwAJt3Fd**
Audio files are also available on streaming services.

Order number: ED 23122
ISMN 979-0-001-20590-0
ISBN 978-3-7957-1523-6
Illustration: Ulrike Müller
Layout: Barbara Brümmer
Editing: Wendy Lampa / Rainer Mohrs
Audio tracks produced and recorded by Ros Stephen
Tuning notes: a = 440 Hz
Piano: Julian Rowlands
Printed in Germany – BSS 59456
© 2023 Schott Music GmbH & Co. KG, Mainz

Contents

1. Violin Junior Song

Ros Stephen

▶ Audio Tracks **1/36**

Teacher's Accompaniment for *Violin Junior Song*

Joyfully

Ros Stephen

2. Tacadie Two-Step

Cajun Two-Step

Ros Stephen

(lower note optional)

Teacher's Accompaniment for *Tacadie Two-Step*

Cajun Two-Step

Ros Stephen

© 2023 Schott Music GmbH & Co. KG, Mainz   ▶ Audio Tracks **2/37**

3. Gavotta in C Major

Play this piece as a duet with your teacher or a friend, or play the top part with the piano accompaniment.

James Hook (1746–1827)
Arr.: R.S.

　▶ Audio Tracks **3/38**

4. Irish Breeze

Peter Mohrs (*1956)

Moderato

▶ Audio Tracks **4/39**

Teacher's Accompaniment for *Irish Breeze*

Moderato

Peter Mohrs

9

5. Zamba de la Luna

The *zamba* is a stately dance from Argentina traditionally performed on guitar and a deep bass drum called a *bombo legüero*. The dancers move in circles, waving white handkerchiefs.

Ros Stephen

▶ Audio Tracks **5/40**

6. Mystery Box

Make up your own melody in bars 5–8 using these notes and note values:

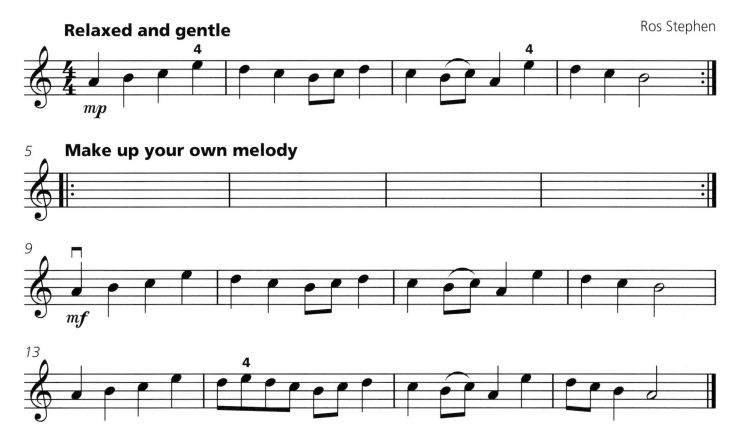

Ros Stephen

Relaxed and gentle

Make up your own melody

Teacher's Accompaniment for *Mystery Box*

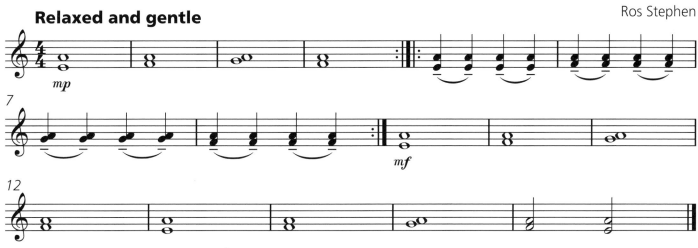

Ros Stephen

Relaxed and gentle

▶ Audio Tracks **6/41**

7. Les Moissoneurs

François Couperin (1668–1733)
Arr.: R.S.

Teacher's Accompaniment for *Les Moissoneurs*

▶ Audio Tracks **7/42**

8. Gavotte in G Major

Georg Philipp Telemann (1681–1767)
Arr.: R.S.

Teacher's Accompaniment for *Gavotte*

▶ Audio Tracks **8/43**

9. Roses from the South

Johann Strauss (Son) (1825–1899)
Arr.: R.S.

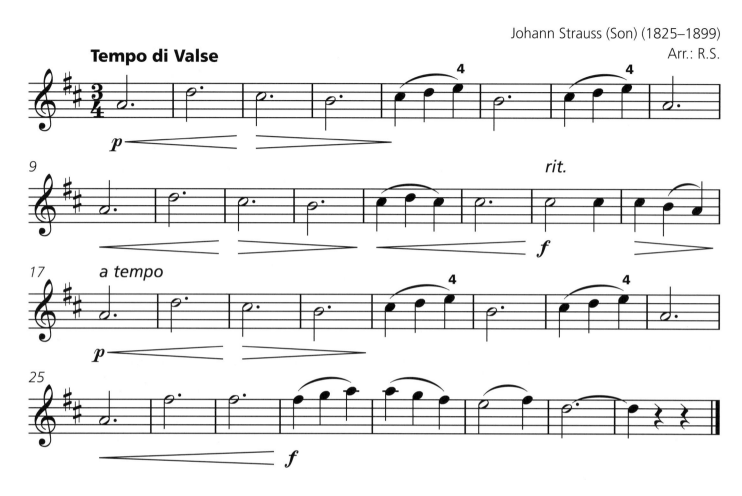

Teacher's Accompaniment for *Roses from the South*

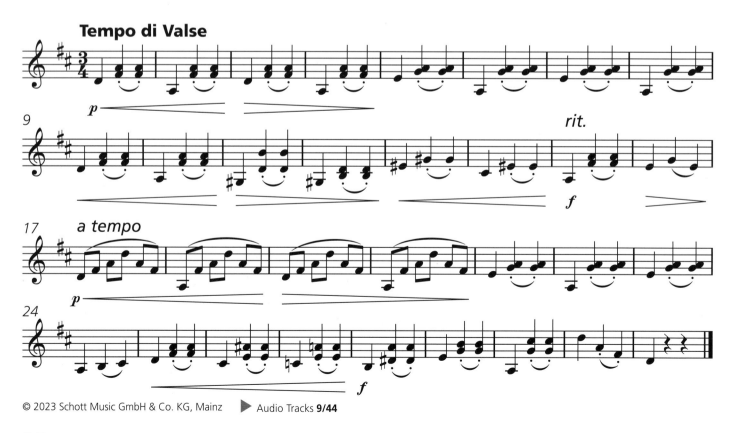

▶ Audio Tracks **9/44**

10. The Enchanted Lady

Trad. Irish
Arr.: R.S.

Teacher's Accompaniment for *The Enchanted Lady*

▶ Audio Tracks **10/45**

11. Milonga de Recuerdos

© 2023 Schott Music GmbH & Co. KG, Mainz ▶ Audio Tracks **11/46**

Teacher's Accompaniment for *Milonga de Recuerdos*

Slow Milonga

Ros Stephen

12. Minuet in G Major

Johann Sebastian Bach (1685–1750)
Arr.: R.S.

Teacher's Accompaniment for *Minuet*

▶ Audio Tracks **12/47**

13. Canon

You can play this piece as a canon with up to four players, or as a solo with the piano accompaniment

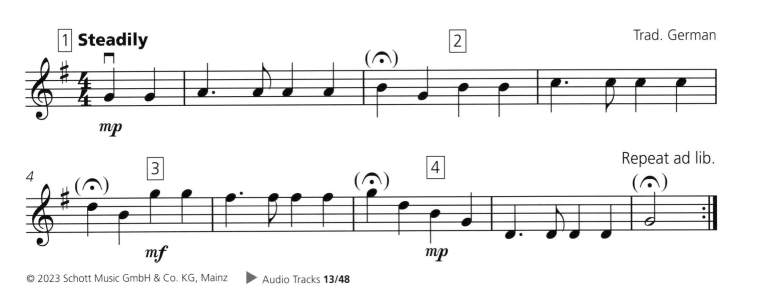

▶ Audio Tracks **13/48**

14. Largo from the New World Symphony

Antonín Dvořák (1841–1904)
Arr.: R.S.

Teacher's Accompaniment for *Largo from the New World Symphony*

▶ Audio Tracks **14/49**

15. Swedish Folk Song

Trad. Swedish
Arr.: Elma and Erich Doflein

Teacher's Accompaniment for *Swedish Folk Song*

Arr.: Elma and Erich Doflein

▶ Audio Tracks **15/50**

16. Zum Gali Gali

You can play this piece as a solo or duet with the piano accompaniment.

Israeli Folk Song
Arr.: R.S.

▶ Audio Tracks **16/51**

Con moto

Arr.: R.S.

17. Have You Seen the Ghost of John?

This canon can be performed with up to four players. Play all the way through without a gap, lower octave, then higher octave, then go back to the start for the repeat. Finish on the pause notes in the 2nd half.

Trad. English Canon

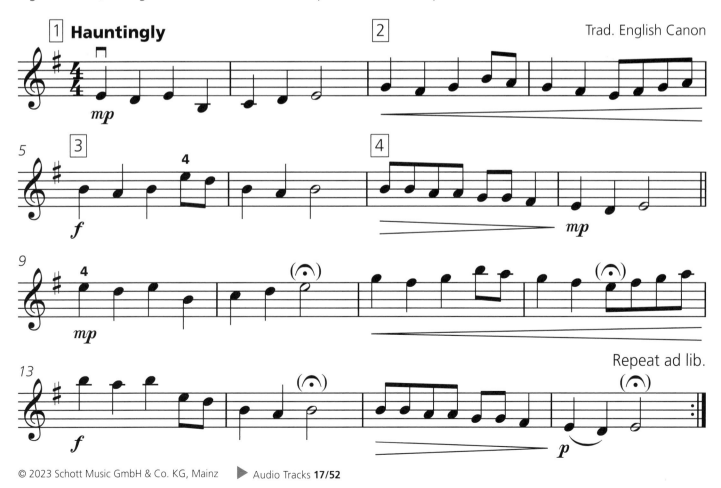

▶ Audio Tracks **17/52**

18. Old Song of Kalevala

This melody is a *Rune* song from Finland. It is traditionally played on a plucked zither called a *Kantele*.
Before you play this piece practise clapping the rhythm while counting to five out loud.

Finnish Folk Song
Arr.: R.S.

▶ Audio Tracks **18/53**

Teacher's Accompaniment for *Old Song of Kalevala*

Arr.: R.S.

19. The Blue Danube

Johann Strauss (Son) (1825–1899)

Arr.: R.S.

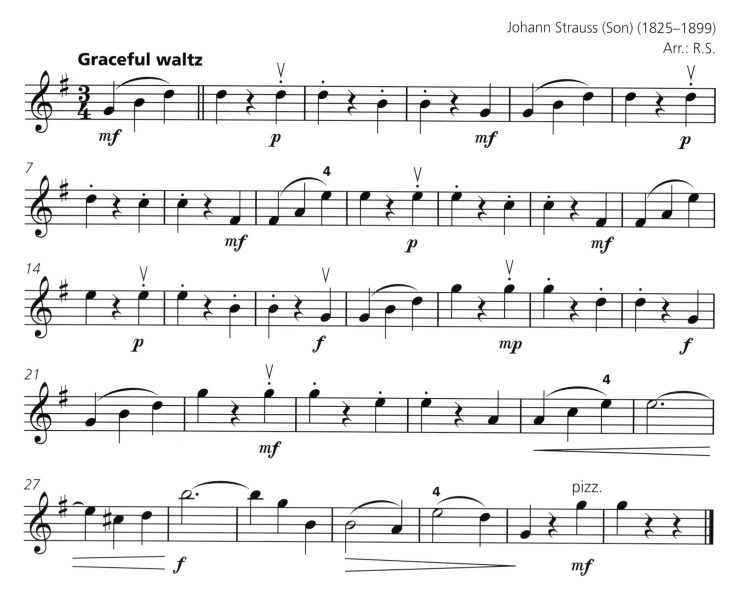

Teacher's Accompaniment for *The Blue Danube*

▶ Audio Tracks **19/54**

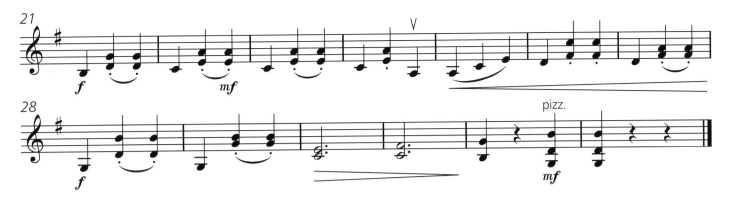

20. Old Joe Clark

Trad. American
Arr.: R.S.

Teacher's Accompaniment for *Old Joe Clark*

▶ Audio Tracks **20/55**

21. William Tell Overture

Gioachino Rossini (1792–1868)
Arr.: R.S.

Teacher's Accompaniment for *William Tell Overture*

▶ Audio Tracks **21/56**

22. Trio from German Dance No. 1 in D Major

You can play this piece as a duet with a friend or play the top part with the piano accompaniment.

Ludwig van Beethoven (1770–1827)
Arr.: R.S.

▶ Audio Tracks **22/57**

FASCINATING FIDDLE FACT

Beethoven is one of the most famous classical composers. He revolutionised classical music, writing pieces that were longer and more complicated than had ever been written before. He continued composing long after he became deaf and played the piano with such passion and intensity that he is said to have destroyed seven instruments!

23. Gavotte in G Major

You can play this piece as a duet with a friend or play the top part with the piano accompaniment.

George Frideric Handel (1685–1759)

Arr.: R.S.

▶ Audio Tracks **23/58**

24. Tumbalalaika

Russian Jewish Folk Song
Arr.: R.S.

Teacher's Accompaniment for *Tumbalalaika*

▶ Audio Tracks **24/59**

25. Gavotte in G Major

Steadily

Esprit-Philippe Chédeville (1696–1762)
Arr.: R.S.

Teacher's Accompaniment for *Gavotte*

Steadily

▶ Audio Tracks **25/60**

26. Theme from Horn Concerto No. 4

K. 495

Wolfgang Amadeus Mozart (1756–1791)

Arr.: R.S.

Allegro vivace

Teacher's Accompaniment for *Theme from Horn Concerto No. 4*

Allegro vivace

▶ Audio Tracks **26/61**

27. Theme from Sonata in A

K. 331

Andante grazioso

Wolfgang Amadeus Mozart (1756–1791)

Arr.: R.S.

▶ Audio Tracks **27/62**

FASCINATING FIDDLE FACT

Mozart was a one of the greatest classical composers. He was born in Salzburg, Austria and composed his first piece of music when he was just 5 years old. He wrote more than 600 compositions in his lifetime, including operas, symphonies, concertos and chamber music.

Teacher's Accompaniment for *Theme from Sonata in A*

Andante grazioso

Arr.: R.S.

poco rall. (2nd time)

28. Allegretto

Niccoló Paganini (1782–1840)
Arr.: Renate Bruce-Weber and R.S.

Teacher's Accompaniment for *Allegretto*

Arr.: Renate Bruce-Weber and R.S.

▶ Audio Tracks **28/63**

29. Spring Canon

Trad. German

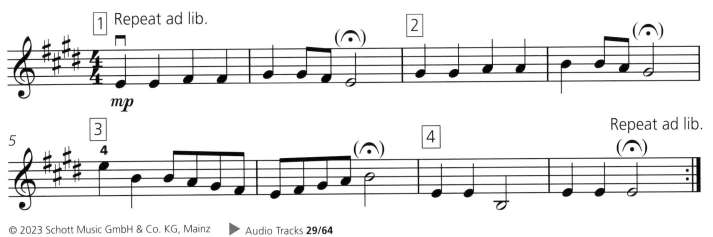

▶ Audio Tracks **29/64**

30. Trio from German Dance in D Major

Joseph Haydn (1732–1809)
Arr.: R.S.

Teacher's Accompaniment for *German Dance*

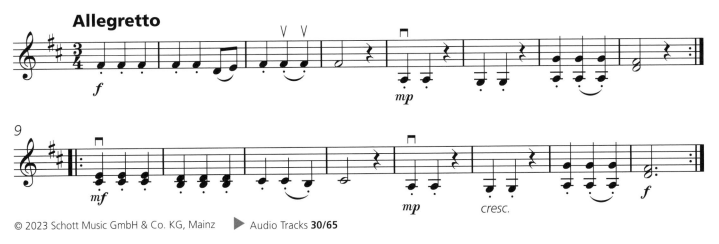

▶ Audio Tracks **30/65**

31. Dance of the Lost Keys

Watch out for the D naturals in this piece!

Lively Jig

Ros Stephen

▶ Audio Tracks **31/66**

Teacher's Accompaniment for *Dance of the Lost Keys*

Lively Jig

Ros Stephen

32. Bog-Down Blues

Try changing some notes and/or rhythms on the repeat.

Ros Stephen

Teacher's Accompaniment for *Bog-Down Blues*

Ros Stephen

▶ Audio Tracks **32/67**

33. Tell Me the Secret!

Ros Stephen

▶ Audio Tracks **33/68**

Teacher's Accompaniment for *Tell me the Secret!*

Con moto

Ros Stephen

34. Hallelujah

Chorus from the Oratorio *The Messiah*

George Frideric Handel (1685–1759)

Arr.: R.S.

▶ Audio Tracks **34/69**

Teacher's Accompaniment for *Hallelujah*

Arr.: R.S.

FASCINATING FIDDLE FACT

The *Hallelujah* chorus is from Handel's great Oratorio *The Messiah*, written in 1741. King George II stood up in the first London performance of the *Hallelujah* chorus, and ever since then it has been traditional for the audience to stand when the *Hallelujah* is performed.

35. Disco Beats

Ros Stephen

▶ Audio Tracks **35/70**

Teacher's Accompaniment for *Disco Beats*

Ros Stephen

Goodbye! See you again in Concert Book 3!